# A NUMBERS GAME

TINAMARIE COX

Nymeria Publishing LLC

First published in the United States of America by Nymeria

Publishing LLC, 2025



Nymeria Publishing

PO Box 350747

Jacksonville, Fl 32235

Visit our website at www.nymeriapublishing.com

Print ISBN 9781969098048

Ebook ISBN 9781969098055

1st Edition

Printed in U.S.A

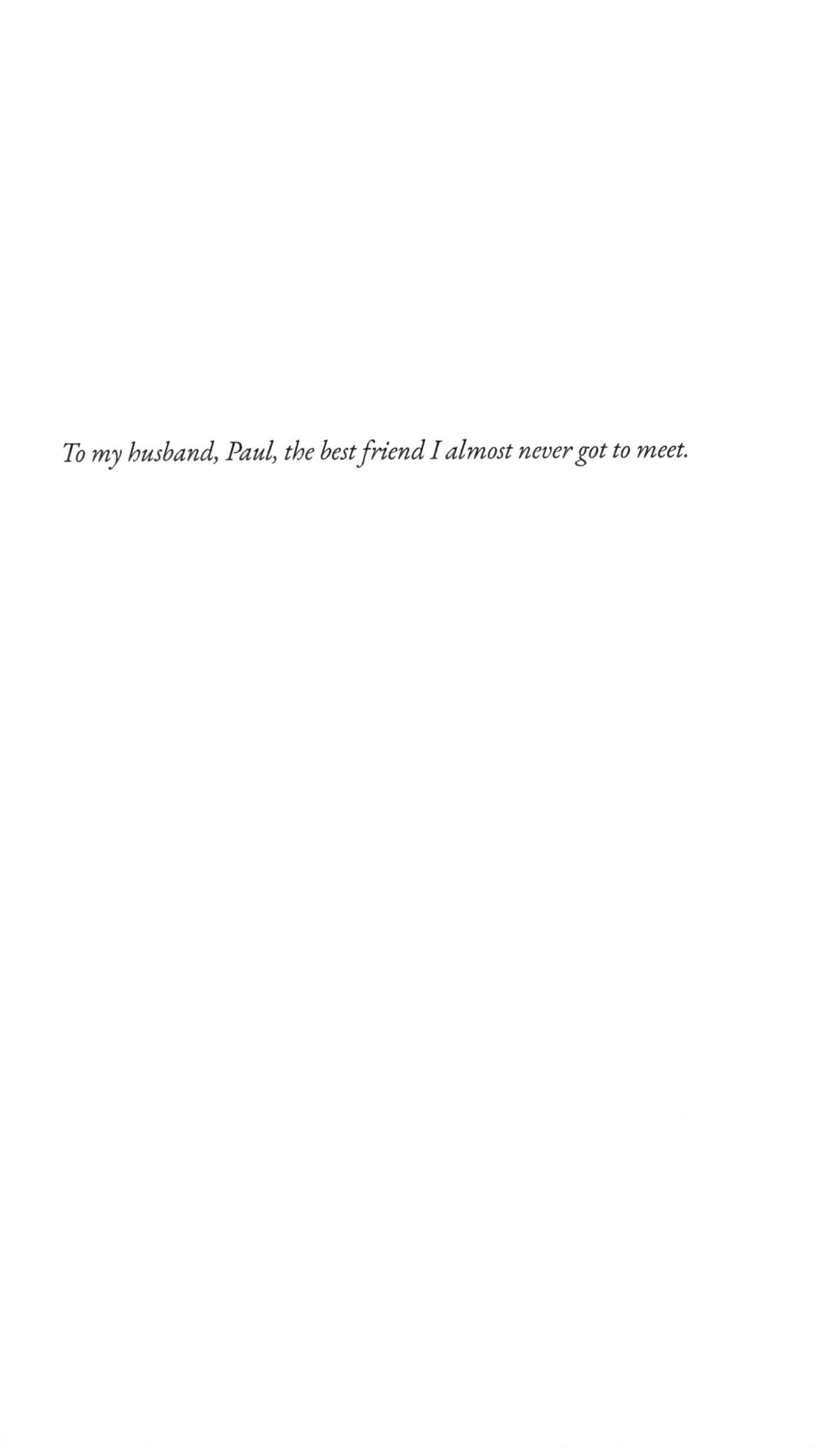

*To my husband, Paul, the best friend I almost never got to meet.*

# Table of Contents

**Part I: A Milestone Reached**

3 The Power Of Numbers
5 Measuring Distance With Time
8 Holding Onto The Rhythm Of A Heart
12 Being Devalued With The Assistance Of A Calendar
18 Black And Purple Are My Favorite Duo
21 Multiple Choice

**Part II: Halves**

28 First And Last
32 Home Is Where The Heart Is, Or Some Kind Of Load Like That
35 Codependent Apple
38 Gifted Child Survival Mode
42 A $6 Disappointment

**Part III: A Change In Scenery**

49 Bubble Pop
54 Haunted
56 Could It Be Worse?
59 The Night I Swallowed
61 One Last Thought For The Road

**Part IV: What Did And Didn't Happen Next**

65 Half-Past
67 Two Vital Numbers
70 The Number 17 Goes Unnoticed
72 Filled By Questions

74 Dancing Sobered
77 Burp
80 I Wish The Words Were Different, But They Weren't
83 Double Standards
86 Creeping Numbers
88 Places Are Nouns, Feelings Are Verbs
90 Time Is Just A Set Of Numbers I Can't Count Along To

**Part V: No Set Number**

95 Coded Messages
97 Points Of View
100 Chaos Tastes Better Than The Truth
103 The Truth Shall Set You Free
106 ; (x2)
108 Assigning Values To Grains of Sand
111 Division
114 Was It Worth The Wait?
116 I'll Never Be Young Again
118 Split In Two
120 A Glimmer

**About the Author**

**2024 Interview with PoetryForMentalHealth.org**

**Text Images Transcribed**

**All words, artwork, and photographs belong to Tinamarie Cox. Publishing credits for specific pieces are noted.*

# CONTENT WARNING

The material within this collection directly coincides with an actual suicide attempt and struggle with mental illness. Inside you will find references to childhood trauma, emotional abuse and neglect, and self-negativity, as well as notes of positivity (because, eventually, the sun does rise). Please read with care if you are sensitive to these and related topics. This is a book of poetry as much as a memoir, and the subject matter may be triggering or upsetting for certain individuals. *A Numbers Game* is a mental health journey described through poems, prose, images, and artwork.

Most importantly, always remember you are never as alone as you feel on your darkest days. If you feel suicidal, there are resources available to help, such as the 988 text/hotline. Don't let suicide be the ending to your story. The present moment will not last forever.

This project was developed as a tool for my healing. Because telling your story matters.

# Part I: A Milestone Reached

*I don't know how to celebrate this milestone.*

*Do I celebrate this milestone?*

"Checked Out," Mixed media canvas, 2023

## The Power Of Numbers

I've unintentionally put a lot of power in a number.

The number **19**.
It seems innocuous, doesn't it?

But it's half my age.
This summer, I turned **38**.

Divide **38** by **2** and you get **19**.
**19** years ago, I was only **19**.
**19** was half a lifetime ago.

Half a lifetime ago doesn't feel that far away.
**19** years doesn't feel that long at all.

Rather than looking forward to the next decade,
I am looking over my shoulder and
obsessing over **19**.

*Pencil drawing: self-portrait, 2021*

*Oil pastels: self-portrait, 2004*

## Measuring Distance With Time

The woman I am<br>
        at **38**<br>
is so different from the girl I was<br>
        at **19**<br>
        the girl who defied her density<br>
                and sank<br>
                and sank<br>
        into a sea laced with midnight hues.

But here<br>
        at **38**<br>
I learned to swim and cut myself loose from anchors<br>
        that dragged me down<br>
                and down<br>
                and nearly drowned me.

The woman I am<br>
the girl I was<br>
        this same body<br>
        this same heart<br>
                and soul<br>
                and yet<br>
how different we are.

A distance of **19** years and a sea apart.

*Pencil drawing (from a 2004 photo at age 19), 2005*

*Photo: Age 19 and a few weeks away from moving day (Staten Island, NY), 2004*

*Digital art self-portrait, 2023, age 38*

## Holding Onto The Rhythm Of A Heart

Even though I don't recognize her anymore,
I'm still afraid to lose her,
afraid to let go,
afraid to no longer be able to feel her.

I've held onto her all this time
because somebody had to love her,
somebody had to know her,
somebody had to feel her.

I am not the girl I was at **19**,
but I am so terrified to never feel her again,
to never hold and comfort her again,
to cease to remember she existed.

So, I remember her
again and again,
feel her pain
again and again,
keep her inside me, alive and close to the surface,
and let her wind through my circulatory system with every beat of my heart
again and again.

*Photo: age 19 (Staten Island, NY), 2004*

*Photo: moving across the country at age 19 (North Carolina stop), 2004*

*Photo: moving across the country at 19 (Texas stop), 2004*

*"Ageing Beauty," mixed media canvas, 2023*
*(published in* Viridian Door Literary, *2024)*

## Being Devalued With The Assistance Of A Calendar

Most of the time
I have trouble relating to other women.
As I approach **40**,
I watch other women dreading rising numbers.
Approaching and surpassing **40** makes them squirm.
Society has made it clear
that women lose their value as they age.
Everywhere we look
the grays are being covered up,
wrinkles painted away,
serums promising to restore our fleeting youth,
and capitalism bankrupting us with lies.
I won't let ad-men
determine my worth or how I should age.
Time is merciless and spares no one.
Age gracefully?
I will go out like a storm.

*Photo: page from my notebook, 2023*

*Photo: page from my notebook, 2023*

*Photo: page from my notebook, 2023*
*(later added to my first chapbook,* Self-Destruction in Small Doses*)*

*Photo: page from my notebook, 2023*

*Pencil drawing: My Combat Boots, 2003*

## Black And Purple Are My Favorite Duo

Fitting neatly into boxes always required me to sever the best parts of who I am.

I am not a delicate femme, but I believe I am still female in my nature:

Without makeup clogging my pores and filling my creases.
Without the latest fashion hugging my softening muscles.
Without a hairstyle considered gentle and feminine.

I don't think diamonds are a girl's best friend.

My house looks like we live here and not a magazine spread.
My decor is mismatched because I like too many different things.

Instead of heels, I live in my Converse sneakers.
Instead of mannequin-worthy tops, I live for snarky t-shirts.

I will choose a burger and fries over fine dining.

Take me to a rock concert for a date,
and let me feel my rage.

*Pencil drawing: Converse high-top sneakers, 2003*

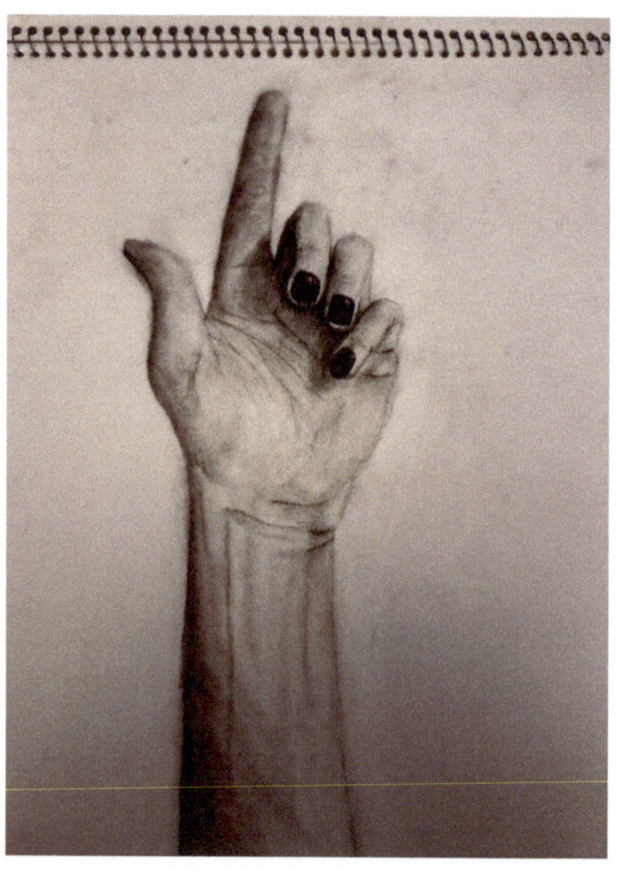

*Pencil drawing, 2003*

## Multiple Choice

At **38**, I found myself at a crossroads, a place where multiple paths diverged and promised different outcomes. I decided to subtract the choices that would continue to take more pieces of ME away. I found the path leading to authenticity, and I am closer to the answer of who I am supposed to be.

*Photo: page from my notebook. 2023*

*Photo: page from my notebook, 2023*

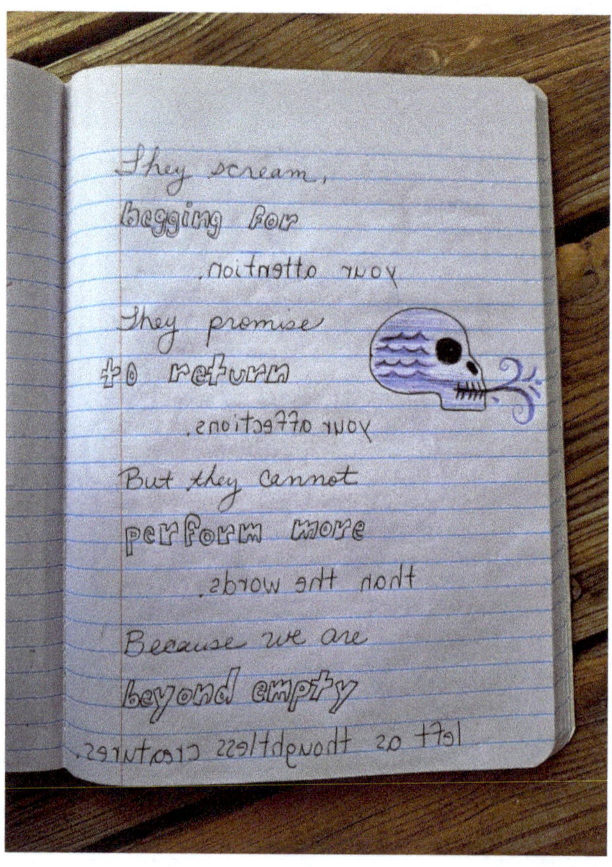


*Photo: page from my notebook. 2023*

*Photo: page from my notebook, 2023*

*Photo: page from my notebook, 2023*

# Part II: Halves

*There is significance in halving my age this year…*

## First And Last

**19 + 19 = 38**

The first **19** years belong to New York.

The second **19** to Arizona.

A balance in numbers.
Equal parts. Years spent equitably.
**2** states.
**2** coasts.
How have I lived so evenly?
I thought there would be more numbers.
As usual, Life had other plans.
She wanted me to live in halves.
She trapped me here.

*Photo: View of the Verrazano Bridge from South Beach, Staten Island, NY (undated/ early 2000s)*

*Photo: looking out at the residential area from our rental home in Prescott Valley, AZ 2004*

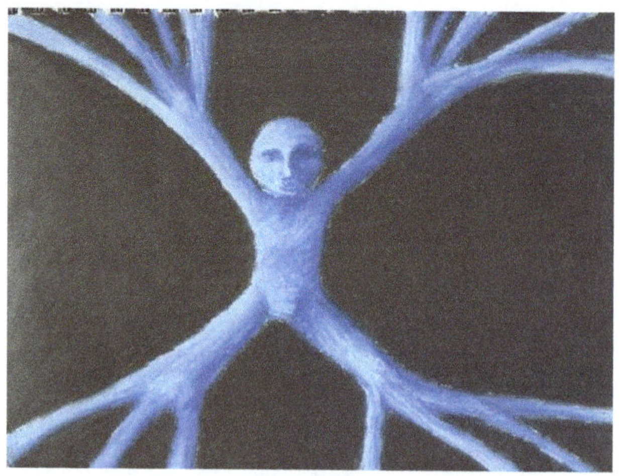

*Oil pastels, 2004*

*Oil pastels, 2004*

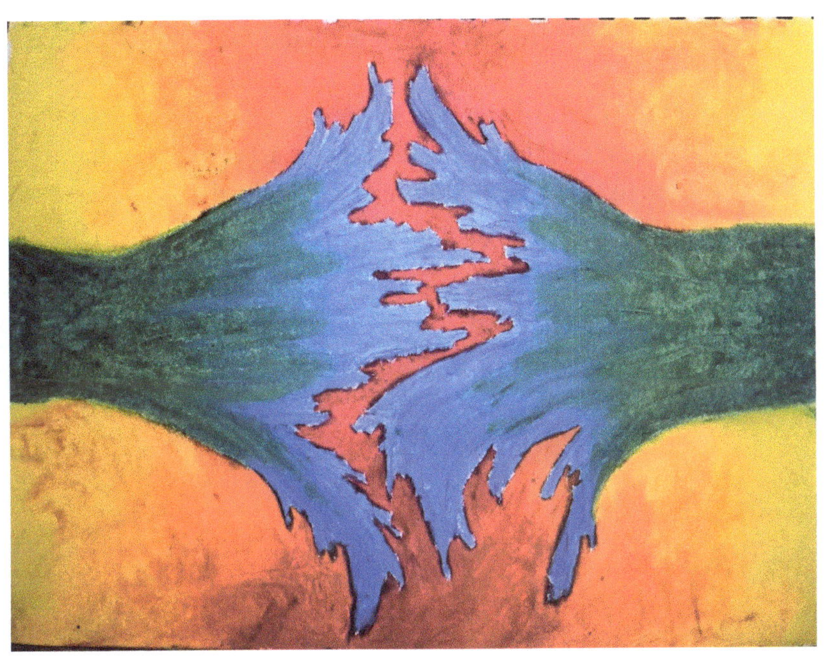

*Oil pastels, 2004*

## Home Is Where The Heart Is, Or Some Kind Of Load Like That

New York wasn't home (despite the **19** years).
Arizona still doesn't feel like home (despite the **19** years).
I just don't feel like I belong in the universe (despite the **38** years).
But where else is there to go (despite the ___ years left)?

*Photo: Childhood home on moving day (Staten Island, NY), November 2004*

*Photo: shared attic/bedroom emptied for moving day (Staten Island, NY), 2004*

*Photo: moved into our rental home, November 2004*

## Codependent Apple

In my last year of being a teenager,
I left my world behind.
A whole world existed beyond New York City.
Part of me knew that, and yet,
I struggled to feel it.

I had dreams of starting fresh,
but also nightmares of staying in the city that never sleeps
alone.
Who was I to conquer skyscrapers?

A mild-mannered girl,
and no hidden powers beyond my humanity.
Only a single, wounded ego.
A loathing for the being of flesh my flickering light called home.

I had to leave
because I had to change.
I had to run
because happiness was **2** thousand miles away.

I went westward.
Stayed connected to the strands of DNA that entwined me.
I was an apple in the bushel, along for the ride,
acting in fear of separation from the tree that grew me.

*Pencil sketch of the attic space shared by 3 siblings (Staten Island, NY), 2003*

*Photo: moving into my first Arizona bedroom (and first time not sharing a room), 2004*

*Oil pastels, 2004*

*Oil pastels, 2004*

## Gifted Child Survival Mode

When the smart kid commits
to bringing home the best grades,
no one ever questions the pressure on the hinges.
I was on fire, racing through flames to please.

You're smart!
You're smart!

And I continued to drain myself
of brain cells and kindling and connections
that should fill a room,
fill my memory.

It was hard to keep earning the applause.

I remained an outsider, unsociable,
but I brought home good grades!
Those fucking good grades.
All the perfect grades they wanted,
expected,
demanded
be attached to my name.
Love was paid for with good grades.

The rest didn't matter.

You're smart!
But you're so smart!

But I'm numb.

*Photo: just another academic award I didn't care about winning, 1998*

*Photo: High School Graduation, National Honor Society, June 2003*

*Pencil drawing: self-portrait (from a photograph at 18), 2003*

*Pencil drawing, 2003*

## A $6 Disappointment

My mother called me a
DISAPPOINTMENT
when I dropped out of college after only **1** semester.
I had been running on fumes since high school,
and no one was replenishing my fuel.
Mother was a taker,
and I was the weakest of the brood.
Because she'd never take candy from her baby.
I was not the baby.
I was destined for middle child syndrome.
Never as good as a first daughter.
Rotten compared to the last apple from the tree.

DON'T RUIN MY SON
with your brittle devil's bones.
WHY CAN'T YOU BE MORE
like the sister you can't compete with?

My mother called me a
DISAPPOINTMENT
when I couldn't keep up;
when I stayed at a job making less than **$6** an hour.
She judged my go-nowhere retail slot without deliberation,
a jury of flying monkeys at her command.
The potential to be anyone was wasted,
used up, burned away, beaten out of me.
The only dream left was to leave.
I could move away from the city and
no one would ever know I was such a
DISAPPOINTMENT
to my loving mother.

The desert was going to be my reset button
and dry out my tears.
No one would know I was a college dropout,
a retail drudge,
such a fucking
DISAPPOINTMENT.

*Photo: at work (Staten Island, NY), 2004*

*Pen drawing on the back of receipt paper, 2004*

*Pencil & pen drawing, 2004*

*Pencil & pen drawing, 2004*

# Part III: A Change In Scenery

*Nothing about me changed with the scenery...*

*Pencil sketch: messy bookcase is the only location for cell signal (Arizona), 2005*

*Pencil sketch: dresser/TV/plant (Arizona), 2005*

*Pencil drawing: my first cellphone (a Nokia classic!), 2004*

## Bubble Pop

There was a culture shock
(naturally),
going from the bright lights and downcast eyes of the big city
to the small-town life where people learned your name.
East Coast versus Southwest.
Battle of ecology;
technology.
There seemed to be more than a time zone difference
(a way of living out of a history textbook),
this town not yet reeking of modern etiquette
(or lack thereof etiquette).
And it turned out that I was invisible no matter where I went.
At first, it was a fascination,
but then the realization that deciduous trees still grow here
(with less of a chance that the human population will wipe you out).
There was a bubble *pop*
(loud and messy),
and then the weight of the open sky began to crush me.

*Photo: The South Beach Pier from the beach, Staten Island, NY (undated/early 2000s)*

*Photo: Entering Northern Arizona, November 2004*

*Photo: Arriving in Prescott Valley, AZ, November 2004*

*Photo: wild cactus in Arizona, 2004*

*Photo: Granite Mountain, as viewed from Thumb Butte (Prescott, AZ), 2023*

*Photo: the saguaro cacti along I-17 North (from Phoenix AZ), 2023*

*Pencil drawing, undated (2004/5)*

## Haunted

It might have still been November
(or maybe it was already December?),
but a number resting in the year **2004**,
and this was when **19** became a thing to haunt me.
A thing not mentioned in my journals boldly,
but lurking in shadows and spaces between lines of poetry.
A slice in my memory.
Half a lifetime ago, I nearly died.

At a time of gratefulness and blessings and good cheer,
I lived in a world painted black for the holiday season.
Half a lifetime ago, I wish I could forget what they did.
Jealous of how they went to sleep without questions
and woke up with blank slates.
How **19** became as invisible as me,
and the girl I was didn't rise the next morning the same.

And I tried to ignore it.
But I marked myself forever
    with my number,
    with my secret,
    with my shame,
    with my trauma.
I entered into a numbers game.

*Pencil drawing, undated (2004/5)*

*Photo: officially an Arizona resident, 2004*

**Could It Be Worse?**

why admit to feeling depressed or having suicidal thoughts when everyone around YOU who is supposed to care won't even try to understand your complex emotions/ like there's something wrong with YOU for not feeling happy and grateful and blessed every damn day/ YOU have to power through that sadness, that debilitating weight, alone/ because everyone has a hard time, you know/ you're not special/ there are plenty of people who have it worse than YOU.

*Oil pastels, 2004*

*Oil pastels, 2004*

*Pencil drawing, 2004*

*"Alone and Empty," acrylic painting, 2023*
*(published in* San Antonio Review, *2024)*

## The Night I Swallowed

I remember that I *broke*,
        but not how many weeks it took to *shatter*.
The decision was quick,
        easily made while everyone slept peacefully
        and I writhed alone in agony.

I remember that I swallowed,
        but not how many pills *tumbled* from the bottle.
The effects of my choice
        overwhelmed me immediately,
        and I *stumbled* from the bathroom to the bedroom.

I remember that I was in disbelief,
        but there was no way to stop it.
The last minutes *slowed* with my heartbeat,
        and suddenly, I was scared.

I remember the clock read **11:34** (pm)
        and how it was too late to change my mind
        and how heavy my body felt being *paralyzed* on the mattress
        and how I couldn't shout for help
        and how I couldn't keep my eyes open.
Everything *blurred* before it turned black.

*Pencil sketch: the bathroom where I swallowed, 2005*

*Oil pastels, 2004*

## One Last Thought For The Road

There is only **1** road a Catholic girl can travel down when she takes too many pills and forgets that holy water bathed her infant head; forgets that someone already died to save her from disgrace.

What was Hell going to be like? **1** last thought stemmed from all the religious pages I was force-fed.

But there was nothing.

No bright light.

No Hellfire,

And no **1** came to rescue me.

The angels had all covered their eyes.

*Pencil & pen drawing, 2004*

*Oil pastels, 2004*

*Oil pastels, undated (2004/5)*

# Part IV: What Did And Didn't Happen Next

*But I didn't die...*

## Half-Past

I had no idea I'd feel so groggy
        after my resurrection.
I had no idea there'd be so much slime on my pillow
        after my kiss with Death.

Have you ever been hungover?
This was **100** times worse than that.

Sensation crept back into my limbs
        like a spider making delicate connections in his web.
My head pounded with the steady rhythm
        of a high school marching band.
Despite my eyes feeling like fuzzballs in my skull,
        I stared at the numbers on the clock
                both curious and afraid
        until the optic nerves had me guessing what the lines meant.

Half-past **4**.
        Half-past **4**?
Confused but grateful.
Whatever prayer I had offered up to the universe
        in those last moments of consciousness
                about not actually wanting to die
        had been answered.

I was alive.
        Alive and ashamed of myself.
        Alive and feeling the stupidest I ever had in all my life.

Why was I still alive?
Here was another example of something I couldn't do right.

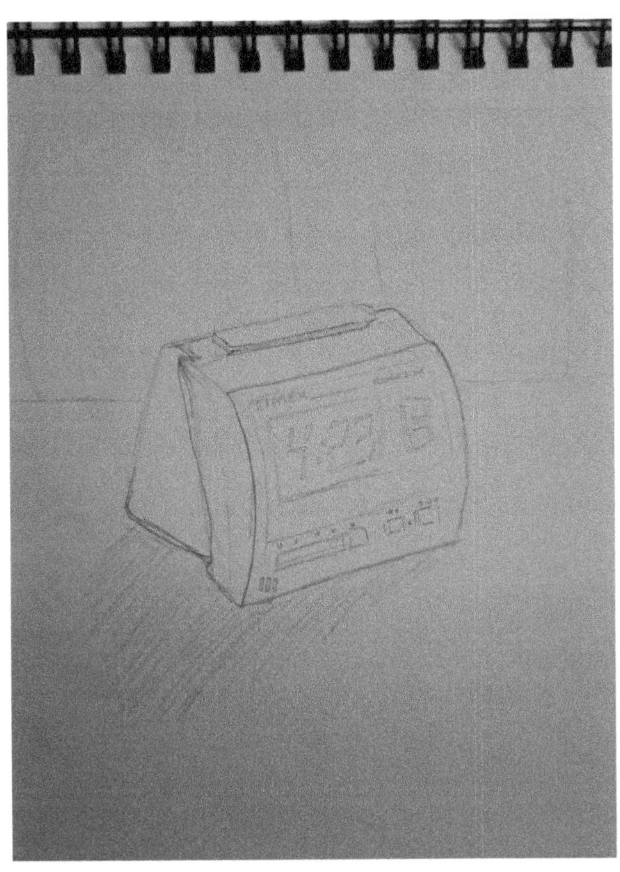

*Pencil sketch: my alarm clock, 2005*

## Two Vital Numbers

I came to the conclusion that I was all alone in my struggles
at **13**.
At **13**,
I decided that I shouldn't bother anyone with my feelings ever again.

At **13**,
I had tried to reach out about my mental health struggles.
I couldn't tell my mother about my deep sadness and dreams of death
at **13**.
At **13**,
my petition to see a psychiatrist was rejected.
I could talk to my mother for free
at **13**.
At **13**,
I should have known she wouldn't help me.

At **9**,
she refused to take me to the doctor to look at my wrist.
I broke my wrist and it took days to convince her the pain was real
at **9**.
At **13**,
I don't know why I thought she would believe my pain then either.

*Photo: class pictures Fall 1994, age 9*

*Drawing: my birthday 1996, age 11*

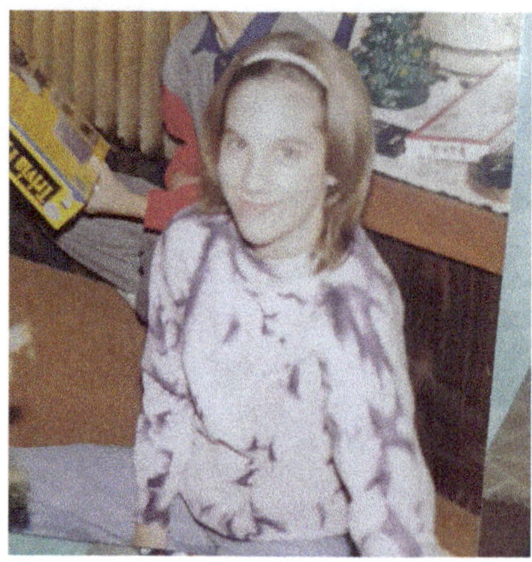

*Photo: putting on a smile for Christmas 1998, age 13*

*Photo: 8th Grade Graduation, June 1999*

## The Number 17 Goes Unnoticed

The fog cleared after I supplied the storm with pills,
and I realized there had not been a morning sun to see.
Half-past **4** was almost **5**
in the evening.
**17** hours had passed between the girl I was
and who remained.
An entire day was spent on a mattress on the floor,
alone and unconscious.
Because no **1** checked in on **19**-year-old me
for a whole day.
There was **0** breakfast,
**0** lunch,
and dinner hour was blossoming.
A person had to eat and drink and use the bathroom at some point
in **17** hours, didn't they?
But I wasn't even a thought.
I was not a daily essential.
Where else would I have been without
friends or a job or a car or any independence?
I was in my bedroom
all night and most of the day,
alone.
That's all anyone cared to know.
And that brought a new kind of pain,
knowing that I didn't matter enough to my family for them to notice
my absence despite my presence.
Maybe I was as worthless as I thought I was.

*Pencil sketch: the view from my mattress on the floor, 2005*

## Filled By Questions

If I had died,
    when would a house full of my family have found my body?
Would someone have come in to get me for dinner?
    Come in to say goodnight?
    Wait until the next morning to care about someone besides themselves?
Would they have mourned me?
Would they have said they never saw the signs I had been exhibiting for nearly a decade?
Would they have complained that I ruined a perfectly good mattress?
    Said I spoiled their first Arizona Christmas experience?
If they hadn't noticed I was gone all day, why bother telling them what happened?
    Could I erase what I did if no one else knew about it?
    Did I need to tell anyone what I was sure I'd never try again?
    Would anyone believe me since I wasn't bleeding or dead?
    Would they write me off as dramatic or attention-seeking?
And if they believed me, what then?
    I heard my mother's voice in my head telling me how stupid I was for trying to kill myself.
    I couldn't imagine my harshest critic saying anything I needed to hear her say.
    I was already a DISAPPOINTMENT, what other words could she use that would hurt more than that?
        I am an inconvenience?
            I am a burden?
                I am a waste of existence?
            I was too fragile to receive more of her judgment.

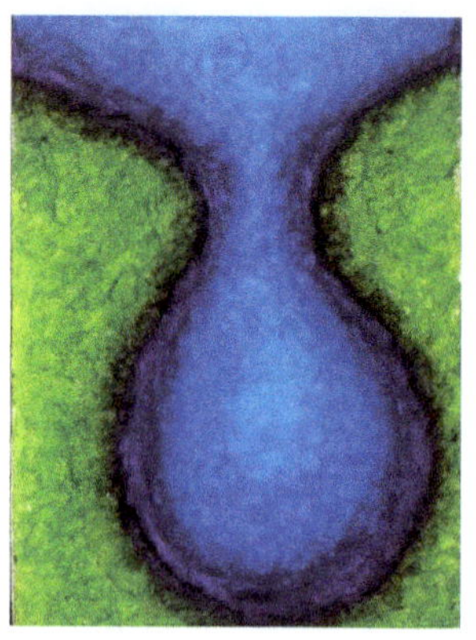

*Oil pastels, 2004*

*Photo: first Arizona snow, December 2004*

## Dancing Sobered

This was not the first time, and
	it would not be the last.

Somedays,
	even half a lifetime away,
I play out a satisfying death in my head.

Still,
	at **19** years old,
it was the closest I'd ever come to an end.

There have been other dances with Death,
	but none where I drank his wine again.

*Photo: pretending everything was fine and starting Community College, 2005*

*Pencil drawing, 2005*

*"Awakening," photography published in* San Antonio Review, *October 2023*

## Burp

The past would not be ignored,
no matter how neatly I packed it away
with all the photographs and cassette tapes and old Band-Aids.

Because, somehow, the subject came up in conversation
with an in-the-moment friend,
and that first taste of empathy on my tongue felt strange.

The fuzzy feeling dripped down my throat
and the warmth settled around my heart.

Grateful I was still here?
What sort of trick was this?

*Oil pastels, 2004*

*Oil pastels, 2004*

*"The Fox Thru Winter," oil painting, 2022*
(*published in* Scavengers Literary Magazine, *2023*)

## I Wish The Words Were Different, But They Weren't

I was riding a wave of courage
and flew too close to the sun.
I told my mother about why the number **19** haunted me.
She said everything I expected to hear,
which was nothing a parent should have said.

*stupid     Stupid STUPID*
*how could you   How Could YOU*
*what about me Me     ME*

This moment was then erased from our record.

*"All Alone Inside My Head," oil paint on canvas, 2023*
(*published in* Poetry As Promised Magazine, *2024*)

*"Mother and Child," oil painting, 2023*
(*published in* Passionfruit Review, *2024*)

## Double Standards

I was never the main character in my story.
I wish I was close to being secondary.
But heartbreak for us tertiary beings
is blurry when you're buried deep in the background.
You're never as bright compared to the other stars.

I never outright asked for empathy,
but a little sympathy would have sufficed.
Like when my younger brother confessed his storm to Mother Superior
and her world came to a screeching halt.
The Reverend Mother always stopped time for the Son
and allowed the rest of the picture to fall to pieces around him.
Any reminder, even small and gentle,
that this type of story was told before in a different voice,
could not overshadow an Only Son on a pedestal.

I had ruined him, too,
once before with my sinful nature, and she would not speak of it.
Those parts of her Good Book where I appear
get altered or erased.
My weathered storms were no exception.
Mother Superior always twisted justice for favored mortals,
kept the scales in her Holy House unbalanced,
and whipped every sentence and judgment down on my back with deaf ears.
*Mercy! Mercy!*
But I can never be redeemed for the shame I brought our name.

*"Blue Girl," oil paint on canvas, 2022*

*Oil paint on canvas, 2022*

## Creeping Numbers

**20**s
**30**s
numbers creeping
rising up as I fall down
        again and again
and why
hindsight is **20/20**
I was never wrong
but wronged
and from my wounds leaked my desires
I was defective
unhappy was how I was meant to be
don't bother anyone
keep your feelings silent
hide inside your cage
play your role if you want to feel love
it isn't that bad
grit your teeth until they go flat
ride every wave of darkness
        again and again
until you drown

*"Sink or Swim," oil paints on canvas, 2023*
*(Published in* Moss Puppy Magazine, *2024)*

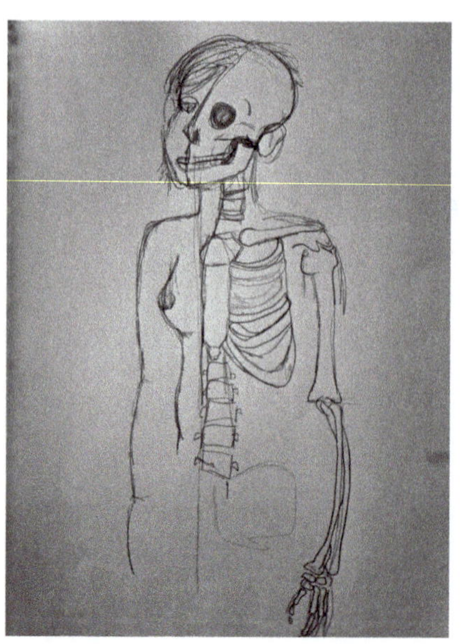

*"It Stays on the Inside," pencil sketch, 2023*

## Places Are Nouns, Feelings Are Verbs

Love isn't in words,
can't be delivered via greeting card.
Love isn't in blood,
can't be carried in veins to a beat.
Love isn't a feeling,
it's a place.
A place without bars.
A place with windows
unlocked and open and letting fresh air in.
Love doesn't run.
Love doesn't judge.
Love doesn't fit neatly into a frame.
It's a place outside my comfort zone.
A place I chose to investigate with a man
who shared his umbrella and his name.

*Erasure poem created for and while dating (my future husband) Paul, 2007*

*Photo: Spring 2007, dating Paul Cox*

## Time Is Just A Set Of Numbers I Can't Count Along To

**14** years married
and I still look for cracks.
I am beside him in our bed,
expecting him to wake up
and realize I'm too much trouble.
I am waiting for him to come to his senses
and figure out there's no hope for us.
I am waiting and watching
for any flags I might find familiar and red.
I am focusing my attention on the hands of the clock
and wondering when I will feel like enough.
I apologize to him
for the things I might not have done yet.

*Photo: Paul and Tinamarie Cox, married for 14 years*

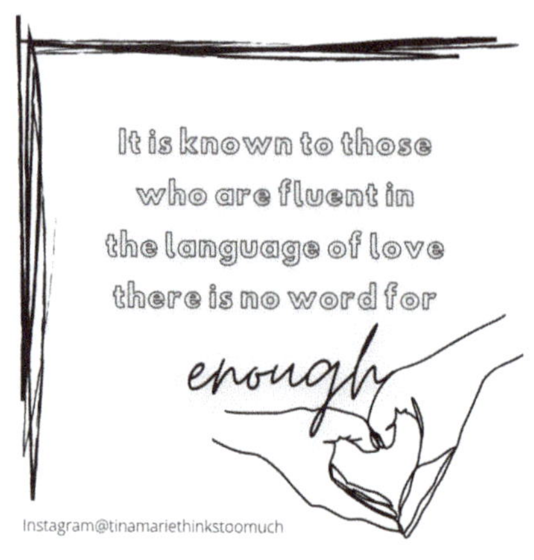


*"enough," Instapoetry, 2023*

## Part V: No Set Number

*Healing is a process.*
*Some days are better than others.*
*There is no set number for recovery time.*

*"The Girl," collage, 2006*

*"Chapter One (with the Narcissist)," Erasure poetry, 2023*

## Coded Messages

The sins of the Father were carried so deeply that they embedded themselves into the DNA– changing my code and the order of the letters that spelled *love*— and condemned us to repeat misspoken words with sharp corners. Here I am, racing against my clock to find a cure, to end the madness, to heal the pattern, and to save my progeny from such a lack of self-awareness.

*"Released," acrylics on canvas, 2023*
*(published with* Soft Star Magazine, *2023)*

## Points of View

I haven't told my family
that I've been going to therapy
or that medication helps me get through the day.
Communication remains our greatest challenge.
We speak different languages under the same roof.
I don't feel heard.
I feel flipped and redirected and rejected.
What's consistent is there's no consistency.
And I find hope in limitations.
Limiting time with those who share my DNA,
forgoing the creation of joined memories,
and accepting that my point of view may never be used.
I find benefits in my new boundaries.
But they only see madness.

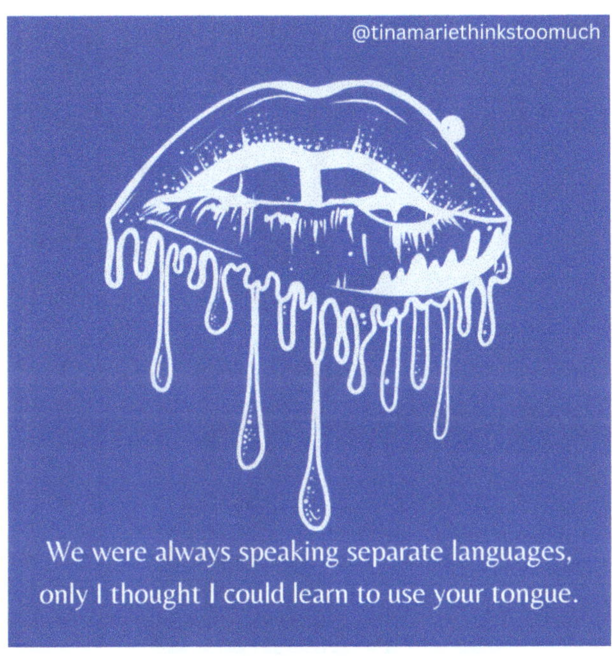


*"Different Languages," Instapoetry, 2023*

*"The Aching Tree," oil paint on canvas, 2023*

## Chaos Tastes Better Than The Truth

Is therapy a violation against mothers?
A conversation of conversion?
A critique on parenting?

My mother boils:
*Therapists always blame the mother.*
She tells us both that she did her best with what she had.

And yes, this could be true,
the sun peeked through the storm clouds and
threw colors at my sky ever so briefly with my reflective tears.
But her best wasn't always something that fed me.
Somedays her spoon was empty.

She mistakes me for pointing a finger
when I hold out the olive branch.

Chaos tastes better than the truth.
The dysfunctional family lives by this unspoken rule,
to live in silent pain.

*"Everyday Living," visual poetry, 2023*
*(Published with* Rinnan Literary, *2023)*

*"Sick in Winter," mixed media canvas, 2023*
(*Published in* Full House Literary, *2023*)

## The Truth Shall Set You Free

I don't want to drag shame around on a leash anymore.
I'm ready to set myself free.
I'll cut loose from this tether with the words I have been avoiding for a lifetime to use.

*Painting: oils on canvas, 2022*

The dream has ended.
The spell is broken.
I've stopped consuming
the sweets you dipped
in poison
to hold me
under your influence.

4

*excerpt from* Little Bouts of Anger *(a visual poetry minizine), 2023*

## ; (x2)

**2** years ago, a friend and I got semicolon tattoos.
I put power in this symbol
        instead of a number.
And I admire the shape on my skin made in permanent ink.
Our stories have not ended**;**
        not yet.

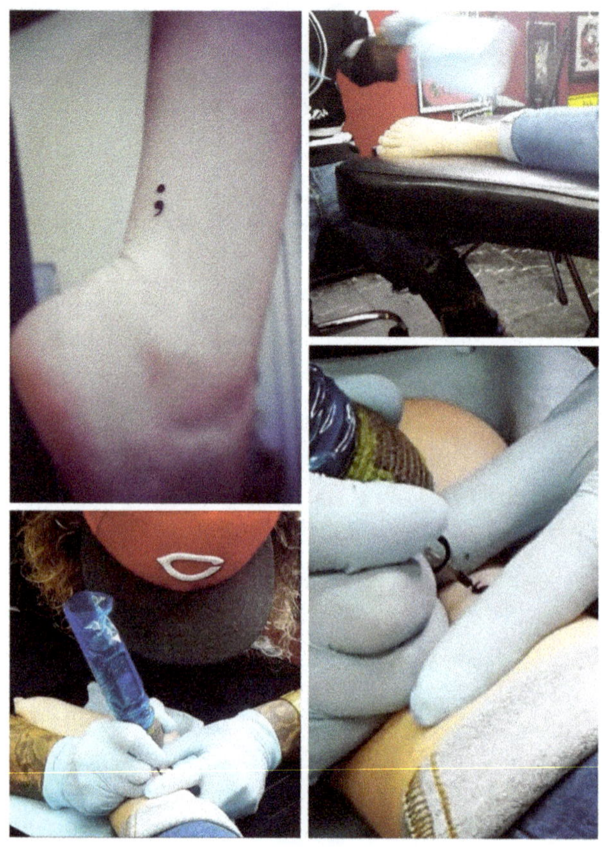

*Photo Collage: freshly tattooed semicolon, September 2021 (with thanks to G.A.E. for being with me & taking pictures)*

## Assigning Values To Grains Of Sand

I was counting the days away like my life was a numbers game, as if somehow assigning values to the grains in my hourglass could lengthen my ledger and save me from myself.

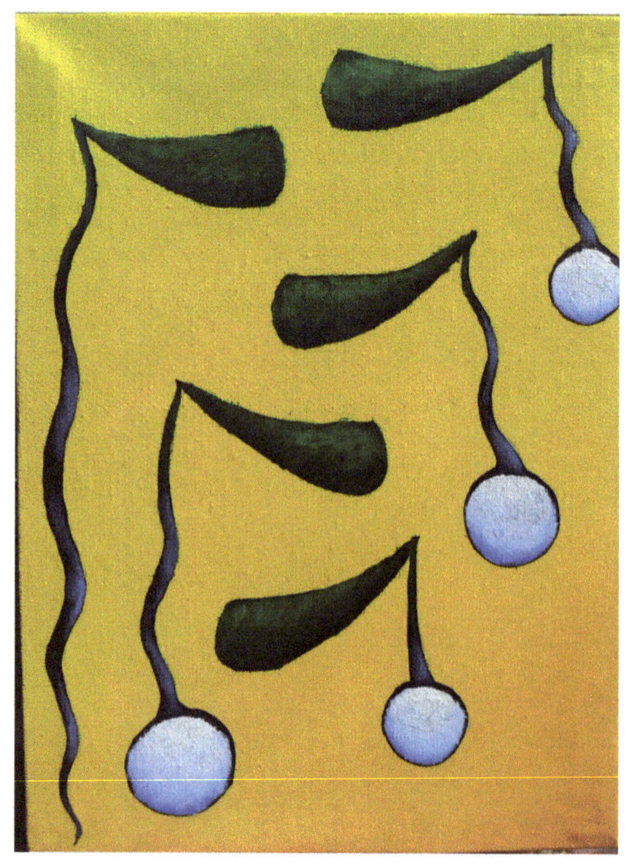

*Painting: oils on canvas, 2022*

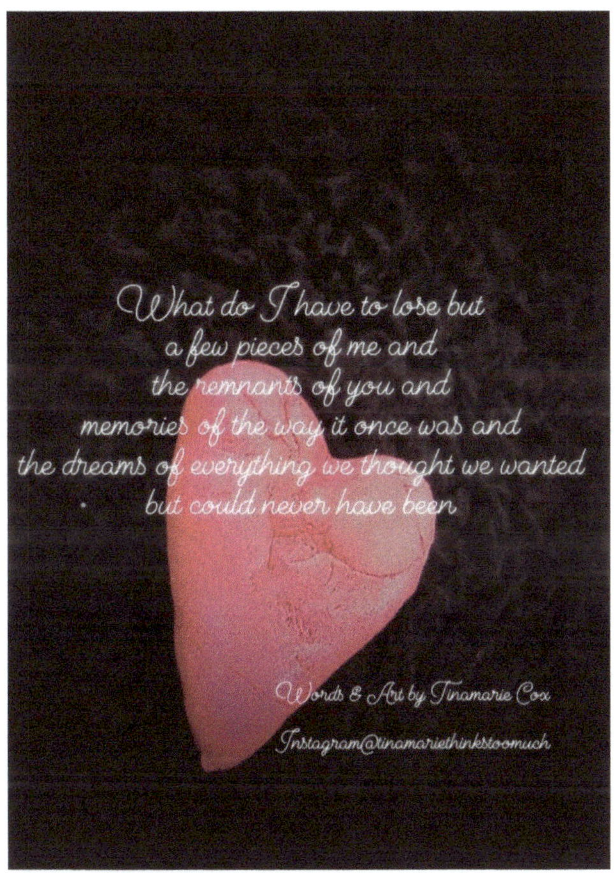


*"What do I have to lose..." Instapoetry, 2023*

## Division

It was division that saved me.
My love for ordinal numbers was a weakness.
I was subtracting my Self
as I struggled to find identity in their mathematic formulae.

As the integers separated,
and the space between the values increased,
somehow I became a stable quotient
among the variables and questionable algorithms.

*Painting: oils on canvas, 2022*

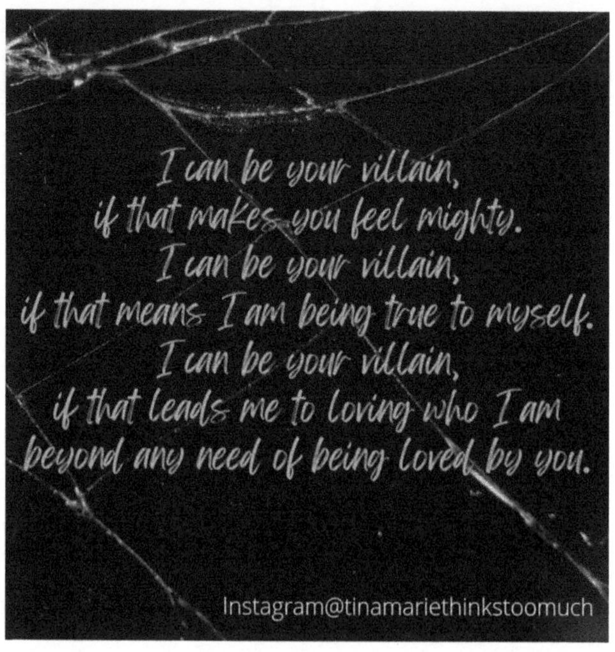


*"The Villain," Instapoetry, 2023*

## Was It Worth The Wait?

**19** years disappeared
from the outside,
but they're still within me,
blending with the sunsets
and sunrises.
Gold and pink and midnight
are colors that remain a part of me.
I was never lost.
I was waiting.

*"The Wait," oil painting, 2022*
(*Published with* Curio Cabinet Magazine, *2023*)

## I Will Never Be Young Again

I'll never be young again,
but perhaps that's the benefit of aging.

I shed the shell I created in my younger days
to become this butterfly
that was almost crushed before it had the chance to pupate.

I learned my greatest enemies stayed close
as they broke my heart one by one.

I grew despite the cuts that turned into scars
and earned the wrinkles around my eyes.

And as I spread my kaleidoscope wings,
I know they will not break because the past
is something I'll never have to live through again.

*"The Loss of Spring," oil paints on canvas, 2023*
*(published in* Moss Puppy Magazine, *2023)*

*Photo: self-portrait, 2023*

## Split In Two

Maybe this is a milestone I will celebrate:
not coloring **38**
    as the **19** years I lost,
    but as the **19** years I was given a second chance to see.
Because I'd give anything to go back **19** years,
    half a lifetime ago,
    and have a **1** to **1.**
To tell the **19**-year-old girl I was
    about the things she will learn over the next half of her life.
Spare her some hard lessons.
Save her from some pain.
Give her what I know now
    for her to compare
    with what she thinks she knows at **19**.
Reassure her that life will be worth living soon.
    Even though some days
    I still need this reminder at **38**, too.

*Photo: celebrating my 19th birthday at a friend's house (Staten Island, NY), 2004*
*(with thanks to E.M.)*

*Digital art self-portrait, 2023*

## A Glimmer

I'd like to catch a glimpse of me at **57**,
and see the picture life has painted me into.
There will be more gray hairs on my head,
and deeper wrinkles around my eyes
(just as there should be).
I will have earned every silver streak,
and each smiling crevice on my face.
In some ways, I will be weaker
but in others, I will have grown stronger.
I will take away the power of numbers.

Numbers will just be numbers,
and not ghosts that haunt me.

*Photo: at a Trivium concert on my 38th birthday, June 2023*

*Photo: at a friend's house (Staten Island, NY) 2004, age 19 (with thanks to A.S.)*

*Photo: the note left in my high school yearbook by my art teacher, 2003*

# ACKNOWLEDGMENTS

The material within this collection directly coincides with an actual suicide attempt and struggle with mental illness. Inside you will find references to childhood trauma, emotional abuse and neglect, and self-negativity, as well as notes of positivity (because, eventually, the sun does rise). Please read with care if you are sensitive to these and related topics. This is a book of poetry as much as a memoir, and the subject matter may be triggering or upsetting for certain individuals. *A Numbers Game* is a mental health journey described through poems, prose, images, and artwork.

Most importantly, always remember you are never as alone as you feel on your darkest days. If you feel suicidal, there are resources available to help, such as the 988 text/hotline. Don't let suicide be the ending to your story. The present moment will not last forever.

This project was developed as a tool for my healing. Because telling your story matters.

## About the Author

**Tinamarie Cox** was born and raised in Staten Island, New York, and moved to a small town in Arizona in 2004. She met her husband in 2007 at the bookstore where she worked, and married her best friend. Together, they are raising two special needs children. When Tinamarie isn't mothering, running a household, or loving on her rescue felines, she writes poetry and short stories. She reads books of every genre and creates art in various mediums. She also enjoys watching movies and going on short nature hikes with her family.

Her previous poetry collection, *Through a Sea Laced with Midnight Hues* (Nymeria Publishing, 2025), also reflected on her mental health struggles. Tinamarie has battled with anxiety and major depressive disorder for most of her life. During her darkest moments, she has been suicidal. And she acted upon those thoughts at the age of 19. Surviving that event had long-term effects, especially since she continued to deny and hide her mental illness until her 30s.

Now, Tinamarie is capable of challenging those thoughts and feelings and utilizes her available supports to work through her MDD and anxiety. Much of her writing revolves around her inner battles and analyzing her past in some way. Poetry has been a healing and healthy coping mechanism for her since she can remember. By publishing her work, she hopes that telling her story helps others with their mental health journeys.

Tinamarie's written and visual work has appeared in numerous publications, both online and in print, under various genres. She is also the author of two poetry chapbooks with Bottlecap Press, *Self-Destruction in Small Doses* (2023) and *A Collection of Morning Hours* (2024). Her first full-length poetry collection, *Through A Sea Laced With Midnight Hues,* with Nymeria Publishing, arrived in 2025.

You can explore more of her work on her website:
tinamariethinkstoomuch.weebly.com.

Facebook/Instagram/Threads/TikTok @tinamariethinkstoomuch
X(Twitter) @tinamarie_cox

## Interview with Poetry For Mental Health, 2024

*(https://www.poetryformentalhealth.org/interview-with-tinamarie-cox)*

**Thank you for chatting to *Poetry for Mental Health*, Tinamarie. Tell me more about the mental health problems you have had, and their history.**

I think my mental health issues started to surface just as I was hitting double digits in age. I remember the inner emotions I experienced around my 11th birthday. I felt deeply sad, not knowing why. I still have the picture I drew that day: a girl in a raincoat crying enough tears to float a boat.

Anxiety was something that already had affected me every day, only I hadn't had the word for it as a child. All I knew was that I spent most of my day terrified of something going wrong, and everything felt unpredictable. I was scared of making incorrect choices or that I'd let someone see my authentic quirky self and tell me how weird I was.

This hypervigilance was something I experienced at school, out with peers, in public settings, and even at home. Home with your family is supposed to be a safe environment, however, for me, it was just as unpredictable, maybe even more so. Home should have been a stable and reassuring space but I missed out on that version of childhood.

I grew up in an emotionally chaotic home trying my best to be invisible while also doing everything I could to please everyone else. My parents were emotionally immature– a term I only learned more about recently– and made me feel as though I was the problem in most situations. I kept quiet about my emotions because I didn't want a lecture about how things could be worse, or how I needed to be more grateful for my parents.

As a teen, it became more difficult to pretend I was okay. Self-care was a huge battle, especially since I was expected to put everyone's needs before mine and not complain. I spent a lot of time alone, avoiding social situations and anything that required my emotional energy. I just didn't have any to spare. I started living to survive.

When I look back on my teenage years, it's undeniable that I had symptoms of depression. Most days, a shower took too much energy. I was tired all the time, and yet I couldn't sleep. I had trouble expressing joy or a genuine interest in anything. Classmates were going out socializing, meeting up during the summer breaks, participating in school events and extra curricular activities, and dating. I only had the ability to show up to school and use my minimal energy to appear a functional human being.

I had to keep up with the high expectations for me at home, constantly compared to my siblings and my parents' younger selves. Despite my lack of a life outside of people-pleasing, my outward symptoms of depression went ignored by those closest to me. I had excelled at masking - to my own detriment. No one could admit that I wasn't a "normal teenager," not even me.

I was diagnosed with anxiety and panic disorder in my early 20s. But it wasn't until my mid-30s that I was brave enough to confront my depression. I was diagnosed with major depressive disorder. Admitting and accepting my mental illness was an affront to everything I had been raised to believe about myself, my family, my emotions, and the dysfunctional patterns I was stuck in.

**How did you feel? How did you cope at the time?**

While I knew something felt "wrong" with me, I didn't understand my feelings. Emotional intelligence was completely nonexistent. I was ingrained with the notion that feelings were for the weak, something that would be mocked and teased for.

My parents were in constant competition with each other, and us children. Nothing I experienced growing up could ever compare to anyone else in my family, especially my parents. Their immaturity and inability to empathize left me feeling like a burden, an inconvenience, and like I was defective for not feeling happy and grateful with my family at every waking moment. I was made to feel as though I owed my parents my complete loyalty, absolute devotion, blind obedience, and never-ending servitude for their bare minimum parenting. Love was withheld from me if I faltered or did not meet their ever-changing standards and expectations.

All of this caused me to hate myself and feel worthless. I sank deep into a cycle of depression that would continue into my late 30s. To this day, I find it nearly impossible to accept any kind of love and praise. It's difficult for me to not only celebrate my achievements, but just to acknowledge them.

It was in my teens that I started using writing and drawing– solitary activities that kept me quiet and easy for my family– to cope with the heavy emotional load. I had given up journaling in junior high school because my older sister was a constant invader of my privacy and boundaries. Somehow, wherever I hid my diary, she'd find it in our shared room, read it, and mercilessly tease me about whatever I had written.

No one came to my defense or rescue in my sibling confrontations. I was convinced I had to hide my feelings and the parts of me that were supposed to define who I was. No one seemed to want to listen to how I felt and when I did speak up, my experiences were constantly invalidated. Not expressing any feelings (besides happiness), unique opinions, or individualistic ideas was how I stayed safe.

On the surface, our family looked average. There were pictures that contained smiles, but when I look back at some of them, I can still feel the pain I buried. Putting on the "everything's fine" show was slowly killing me.

At around 13, I asked my mom if I could talk to a psychologist and was denied. It was rare that my mom was willing to spend any money, or her emotional energy, on me back then. She told me that if I wanted to talk to someone, I could talk to her for free. But I think she feared an outsider finding out we were not the shiny, happy people we appeared to be; discovering how our family functioned from behind closed doors.

Any light that didn't reflect the image of an ideal family was a threat. That is one of the biggest rules of the dysfunctional family: Keep the dysfunction a secret at all costs, even if it costs your mental and emotional health.

By the time I turned 19, I was utterly broken, numb and hopeless. I became a suicide-attempt survivor. But my near-death experience went unnoticed by my family despite us living under the same roof. And I was so embarrassed and ashamed of myself for attempting suicide, I couldn't bring attention to what I'd done either. Even when I tried to talk about it years later, my mental health struggles were still not fully accepted. Anything that didn't fit neatly into the smiling box was shamed and submerged. I didn't know how to escape. I didn't think I ever would.

My anxiety, depression, and suicidal ideation went on being ignored, even by myself, and therefore, went untreated for many years. I suffered through depleting panic attacks, sank deep into depressive episodes, danced with suicidal thoughts, and reminded myself I was supposed to be happy. Family loves you, why would they hurt you? I tried to rationalize my emotions. I was convinced there wasn't anything wrong with my family, just me. I told myself I didn't need help. I just had to survive my mind and emotions. I had to keep wearing a mask and keeping secrets.

**What do you do, or have done to cope?**

I tried therapy for the first time in my life only a couple of years ago. Eighteen years after my near suicidal-death, I reached a point where my depressive episodes were, again, significantly affecting my everyday life. I had truly believed I could fake it until I made it. Many of my days had blended together and life felt pointless. Happy moments came and went without the ability to enjoy them. I feel like I missed out on fully experiencing many of life's rights of passage because I was consumed by my mental illness.

I wasn't the mom I wanted to be. I wanted my kids to have a better mother than mine. I wasn't the wife I felt my husband deserved. I didn't want a marriage like my parents. I felt like a hindrance to everyone else's happiness. I tried to put all my energy into my kids and continued to feel empty inside. As much as I loved my children, I didn't love me. I was alive but still not living.

Therapy took some getting used to. Finding a therapist I felt comfortable with was a challenge. I quickly realized I didn't know how to talk about myself because I didn't know myself. Everything I was had been a persona I created to please others and meet the expectations of my family of origin. After several months, I began to rediscover myself and explore the parts of me I had buried.

When I decided to embark on my healing journey, I started journaling again. Now that I lived in a home where I felt safe and could have boundaries, it was easier to spill my thoughts onto paper. I have a husband that I trust and is supportive, who has loved me through my ups and my very deep downs.

Eventually, I added medication to my mental health regimen. I was aware that I needed more support and it is a decision I have no regrets or embarrassment about. I still have anxiety and depression, but they have become manageable. Combined with my therapy, I know that my feelings are not going to last. I know I can talk to someone. I know I can have my medications adjusted. I feel like a better mom and wife because I feel better.

Cutting out the toxicity of my family of origin was more beneficial than I could have imagined. To say it was painful to recognize, acknowledge, accept, and leave my unhealthy roots behind would be an understatement. However, it was completely necessary for my healing and growth into my authentic self. All my life I had believed I was the problem and sacrificed who I was in order to feel some semblance of love. Choosing me felt selfish at first. Now, I know otherwise. I know that I am worthy of love, respect, and empathy. I know I deserved better and I will no longer settle for less. I feel like a new person and I am having an amazing time getting to know her.

**When did you start using poetry to help you?**

A lot of "terrible" poetry came out of my teenage years. But at that time, I wasn't writing to be published or recognized for my work. My poetry was purely an outlet, something private. I kept much of my writing and creativity a secret. My family was heavily critical and judgemental of everything I did. My notebooks and sketchbooks were the "therapist" my mother refused to take me to see. Notebooks wouldn't mock me, judge me, or share my secrets. I could be anyone I wanted on a page of paper.

I left poetry behind after college. As much as I loved composing poems and stories, I had it drilled into my head that I couldn't take that anywhere and I wasn't that good at it anyway. So, I thought I had "grown up" by focusing on a career and building a family. The things we are told from childhood to covet.

Many years later, I rediscovered my love for writing poetry through journaling as an adult. Feelings that overpowered a journal entry often became a series of poems. And sometimes I skipped a long-winded journal entry and opted for a burst of emotional poems instead. Putting my thoughts and emotions into words on a page was a natural part of me. I was finally ready to acknowledge that and embrace it fully.

I always wanted to be published and share my work with others but my anxiety and depression would get the best of me. With my husband's encouragement and my new found sense of self, I started to submit pieces to various publications. There was definitely a learning curve and I got a lot of rejections at the beginning. But for once in my life, I wasn't going to give up on something that was important to me.

Poetry has not only been a healthy way for me to cope, it has also helped me connect with people. I still tend to be a loner, not wanting to drain my emotional energy before taking the necessary time to care for my needs. I continue to need space to explore my unique self so I can live more authentically. Becoming aware of who I am at my core versus who I was told to be has been quite a journey. Poetry has also helped me process how my past has affected me. It's healed some of those wounds handed down to me by my family of origin.

Writing poetry has helped me to be active in my recovery from anxiety, depression, suicide, and people-pleasing. It has taught me self-compassion and made me self-aware when it comes to my own behaviors. I feel as though writing has brought me to a healthier place within myself, and that's something I want to share with others. I want readers to find the best parts of themselves, too, and celebrate their battles as much as their successes.

By publishing my poetry, I believe I am showing others who struggle with their mental health that they are not alone. That their feelings are valid. That they are not broken or helpless or hopeless. Emotions are neither positive nor negative, they simpler are. And experiencing emotions is normal.

**Where has your poetry been published?**

I have been lucky enough to have my poetry appear in many different literary publications and anthologies (such as Poetry For Mental Health's first volume of *Mental Health Anthology*), as well as in book format. Last year, I published my first poetry chapbook, *Self-Destruction in Small Doses, with Bottlecap Press*. This collection of micro-poetry is mental health-related and takes the reader into the depressive and self-destructive thoughts many struggling with mental illness have experienced. My second chapbook, *A Collection of Morning Hours*, still pulls on those existential/who am I/what is life about sort of vibes, but in a lighter way. I don't think this particular chapbook would have been possible without the assistance of therapy and medication helping me to appreciate nature, opportunity, and myself.

My first full-length poetry collection, *Through a Sea Laced with Midnight Hues*, will be released with Nymeria Publishing. These poems are extremely personal and directly correlate with one of my depressive episodes. I noticed that many of the poems I wrote at my lowest referred to the ocean, sinking, and drowning. I was able to trace a journey through my major depressive disorder via my work. This collection of poems is special because it puts words to feelings many people have trouble articulating. I want it to inspire hope for those who are at odds with their mental health, as well as understanding and compassion from the loved ones in their lives.

## Text Images Transcribed

"Checked Out" (pg 2)
Paper Library Checkout Card with various dates
Text sourced from Jane Austen's *Sense and Sensibility*
*He was lightheaded at the time. Had he been in his right senses, he could not have thought of such a thing.*

2023 Notebook Pages
(pg 13)*Splat! You've stepped on me again... I'm sorry. I was in your way. It was my fault. It always is.*
(pg 15) *It is my fears that tear into my soul and give me the justification to hate my name.*
(pg 16) *Tear ducts overworked, your emotion is now void.*
(pg 22) *I wait for better days, but will they ever come or am I a fool just full of vain hopes and useless dreams?*
(pg 24) *They scream/ begging for your attention/ They promise to return your affections/ But they cannot perform more than the words/ Because we are beyond empty/ left as thoughtless creatures*
(pg 25) *When I was younger, I believed in fairies because I wanted to believe something magical could save me when my prayers remained unanswered.*

"Share the Experience" Erasure Poetry (pg 89)
*nothing gives us more pleasure than that we have loved/ and finding gives us the greatest pleasure of all/ provides us with the opportunity to share/ each one is sure our selection was first a story of romantic suspense/ choices have been a work combining the emotional depths of the most intimate drama in a single unforgettable voice/ riveting/ exceptional/ worthy/ stimulating*

"enough" (pg 91)

*It is known to those who are fluent in the language of love there is no word for enough.*

"Chapter 1 (of The Narcissist), (pg 94)
erasure text sourced from *Sense and Sensibility* by Jane Austen
*family was property and constant companion to supply his house/ and he intended constant attention to his wishes which his marriage amply provided for/ soon afterwards, he added to that property/ and their father was also secured to her child*

"Different Languages" (pg 98)
*We were always speaking separate languages, only I thought I could learn to use your tongue.*

"Everyday Living" (pg 101)
*you can't spend every day living/ while keeping your eyes shut*

untitled (pg 105)
*The dream has ended. The spell is broken. I've stopped consuming the sweets you dipped in poison to hold me under your influence.*

"What do I have to lose..." (pg 110)
*What do I have to lose but/ a few pieces of me and/ the remnants of you/ and memories of the way it once was and/ the dreams of everything we thought we wanted but/ could never have been.*

"The Villain" (pg 113)
*I can be your villain, if that makes you feel mighty/ I can be your villain, if that means I am being true to myself/ I can be your villain, if that leads me to loving who I am beyond any need of being loved by you*

2003 High School Yearbook Inscription (pg 122)
*Tinamarie, Pursue the arts!! Your work is always so lovely. It's been a pleasure- Ms Emily Smith*

www.ingramcontent.com/pod-product-compliance
Ingram Content Group UK Ltd.
Pitfield, Milton Keynes, MK11 3LW, UK
UKHW021836270726
14058UKWH00002B/180